R. S. THOMAS

SELECTED POEMS
1946-1968

Also available

POETRY BY R.S. THOMAS

What is a Welshman? (Christopher Davies, 1974)
Between Here and Now (Macmillan, 1981)
Later Poems (Macmillan, 1984)
Ingrowing Thoughts (Poetry Wales Press, 1985)

PROSE BY R.S. THOMAS

Selected Prose, ed. Sandra Anstey (Poetry Wales Press, 1983)
Neb, ed. Gwenno Hywyn (Gwasg Gwynedd, 1985)

ESSAYS ON R.S. THOMAS

Critical Writings on R.S. Thomas, ed. Sandra Anstey
   (Poetry Wales Press, 1983)

R. S. Thomas

SELECTED
POEMS
1946~1968

BLOODAXE BOOKS

This edition published 1986 by
Bloodaxe Books Ltd,
P.O. Box 1SN,
Newcastle upon Tyne NE99 1SN.

ISBN: 0 906427 96 7

First published in Great Britain by Hart-Davis, MacGibbon Ltd 1973
reissued by Granada Publishing Ltd 1979.
Copyright © R.S. Thomas
1946, 1952, 1953, 1955, 1958, 1961, 1963; 1966, 1968, 1973, 1986

Bloodaxe Books Ltd acknowledges
the financial assistance of Northern Arts.

Typesetting by True North, Newcastle upon Tyne.

Printed in Great Britain by
Bell and Bain Ltd., Glasgow

Contents

NOT THAT HE BROUGHT FLOWERS (1968)

SONG AT THE YEAR'S TURNING
(1955)

A Peasant

Iago Prytherch his name, though, be it allowed,
Just an ordinary man of the bald Welsh hills,
Who pens a few sheep in a gap of cloud.
Docking mangels, chipping the green skin
From the yellow bones with a half-witted grin
Of satisfaction, or churning the crude earth
To a stiff sea of clods that glint in the wind —
So are his days spent, his spittled mirth
Rarer than the sun that cracks the cheeks
Of the gaunt sky perhaps once in a week.
And then at night see him fixed in his chair
Motionless, except when he leans to gob in the fire.
There is something frightening in the vacancy of his mind.
His clothes, sour with years of sweat
And animal contact, shock the refined,
But affected, sense with their stark naturalness.
Yet this is your prototype, who, season by season
Against siege of rain and the wind's attrition,
Preserves his stock, an impregnable fortress
Not to be stormed even in death's confusion.
Remember him, then, for he, too, is a winner of wars,
Enduring like a tree under the curious stars.

Night and Morning

One night of tempest I arose and went
Along the Menai shore on dreaming bent;
The wind was strong, and savage swung the tide,
And the waves blustered on Caernarfon side.

But on the morrow, when I passed that way,
On Menai shore the hush of heaven lay;
The wind was gentle and the sea a flower,
And the sun slumbered on Caernarfon tower.

(*From the Welsh Traditional*)

The Cry of Elisha after Elijah

The chariot of Israel came,
And the bold, beautiful knights,
To free from his close prison
The friend who was my delight;
Cold is my cry over the vast deep shaken,
Bereft was I, for he was taken.

Through the straight places of Baca
We went with an equal will,
Not knowing who would emerge
First from that gloomy vale;
Cold is my cry; our bond was broken,
Bereft was I, for he was taken.

Where, then, came they to rest,
Those steeds and that car of fire?
My understanding is darkened,
It is no gain to enquire;
Better to await the long night's ending,
Till the light comes, far truths transcending.

I yield, since no wisdom lies
In seeking to go his way;
A man without knowledge am I
Of the quality of his joy;
Yet living souls, a prodigious number,
Bright-faced as dawn, invest God's chamber.

The friends that we loved well,
Though they vanished far from our sight,
In a new country were found
Beyond this vale of night;
O blest are they, without pain or fretting
In the sun's light that knows no setting.

(*From the Welsh of Thomas Williams, Bethesda'r Fro*)

Song for Gwydion

When I was a child and the soft flesh was forming
Quietly as snow on the bare boughs of bone,
My father brought me trout from the green river
From whose chill lips the water song had flown.

Dull grew their eyes, the beautiful, blithe garland
Of stipples faded, as light shocked the brain;
They were the first sweet sacrifice I tasted,
A young god, ignorant of the blood's stain.

Song

Wandering, wandering, hoping to find
The ring of mushrooms with the wet rind,
Cold to the touch, but bright with dew,
A green asylum from time's range.

And finding instead the harsh ways
Of the ruinous wind and the clawed rain;
The storm's hysteria in the bush;
The wild creatures and their pain.

Welsh Landscape

To live in Wales is to be conscious
At dusk of the spilled blood
That went to the making of the wild sky,
Dyeing the immaculate rivers
In all their courses.
It is to be aware,
Above the noisy tractor
And hum of the machine
Of strife in the strung woods,
Vibrant with sped arrows.
You cannot live in the present,
At least not in Wales.
There is the language for instance,
The soft consonants
Strange to the ear.
There are cries in the dark at night
As owls answer the moon,
And thick ambush of shadows,
Hushed at the fields' corners
There is no present in Wales,
And no future;
There is only the past,
Brittle with relics,
Wind-bitten towers and castles
With sham ghosts;
Mouldering quarries and mines;
And an impotent people,
Sick with inbreeding,
Worrying the carcase of an old song.

Soil

A field with tall hedges and a young
Moon in the branches and one star
Declining westward set the scene
Where he works slowly astride the rows
Of red mangolds and green swedes
Plying mechanically his cold blade.

This is his world, the hedge defines
The mind's limits; only the sky
Is boundless, and he never looks up;
His gaze is deep in the dark soil,
As are his feet. The soil is all;
His hands fondle it, and his bones
Are formed out of it with the swedes.
And if sometimes the knife errs,
Burying itself in his shocked flesh,
Then out of the wound the blood seeps home
To the warm soil from which it came.

The One Furrow

When I was young, I went to school
With pencil and foot-rule
Sponge and slate,
And sat on a tall stool
At learning's gate.

When I was older, the gate swung wide;
Clever and keen-eyed
In I pressed,
But found in the mind's pride
No peace, no rest.

Then who was it taught me back to go
To cattle and barrow,
Field and plough;
To keep the one furrow,
As I do now?

The Minister

Sŵn y galon fach yn torri

Characters
>   NARRATOR
>   DAVIES
>   THE MINISTER
>   BUDDUG

The Minister was broadcast on the Welsh Regional
programme of the BBC in 1952.

NARRATOR

In the hill country at the moor's edge
There is a chapel, religion's outpost
In the untamed land west of the valleys,
The marginal land where flesh meets spirit
Only on Sundays and the days between
Are mortgaged to the grasping soil.

This is the land of green hay
And greener corn, because of the long
Tarrying of winter and the late spring.
This is the land where they burn peat
If there is time for cutting it,
And the weather improves for drying it,
And the cart is not too old for carrying it
And doesn't get stuck in the wet bog.

This is the land where men labour
In silence, and the rusted harrow
Breaks its teeth on the grey stones.
Below, the valleys are an open book,
Bound in sunlight; but the green tale
Told in its pages is not true.

'Beloved, let us love one another,' the words are blown
To pieces by the unchristened wind
In the chapel rafters, and love's text
Is riddled by the inhuman cry
Of buzzards circling above the moor.
Come with me, and we will go
Back through the darkness of the vanished years
To peer inside through the low window
Of the chapel vestry, the bare room
That is sour with books and wet clothes.

They chose their pastors as they chose their horses
For hard work. But the last one died
Sooner than they expected; nothing sinister,
You understand, but just the natural
Breaking of the heart beneath a load
Unfit for horses. 'Ay, he's a good 'un,'
Job Davies had said; and Job was a master
Hand at choosing a nag or a pastor.

And Job was right, but he forgot,
They all forgot that even a pastor
Is a man first and a minister after,
Although he wears the sober armour
Of God, and wields the fiery tongue
Of God, and listens to the voice
Of God, the voice no others listen to;
The voice that is the well-kept secret
Of man, like Santa Claus,
Or where baby came from;
The secret waiting to be told
When we are older and can stand the truth.

O, but God is in the throat of a bird;
Ann heard Him speak, and Pantycelyn.
God is in the sound of the white water
Falling at Cynfal. God is in the flowers
Sprung at the foot of Olwen, and Melangell
Felt His heart beating in the wild hare.
Wales in fact is His peculiar home,
Our fathers knew Him. But where is that voice now?
Is it in the chapel vestry, where Davies is using
The logic of the Smithfield?

DAVIES

A young 'un we want, someone young
Without a wife. Let him learn
His calling first, and choose after
Among our girls, if he must marry.
There's your girl, Pugh; or yours, Parry;
Ministers' wives they ought to be
With those white hands that are too soft
For lugging muck or pulling a cow's
Tits. But ay, he must be young.
Remember that mare of yours, John?

Too old when you bought her; the old sinner
Had had a taste of the valleys first
And never took to the rough grass
In the top fields. You could do nothing
With her, but let her go her way.
Lucky you sold her. But you can't sell
Ministers, so we must have a care
In choosing. Take my advice,
Pick someone young, and I'll soon show him
How things is managed in the hills here.

NARRATOR

Did you notice the farm on the hill side
A bit larger than the others, a bit more hay
In the Dutch barn, four cows instead of two?
Prosperity is a sign of divine favour:
Whoever saw the righteous forsaken
Or his seed begging their bread? It even entitles
A chapel deacon to a tame pastor.

There were people here before these,
Measuring truth according to the moor's
Pitiless commentary and the wind's veto.
Out in the moor there is a bone whitening,
Worn smooth by the long dialectic
Of rain and sunlight. What has that to do
With choosing a minister? Nothing, nothing.

Thick darkness is about us, we cannot see
The future, nor the thin face
Of him whom necessity will bring
To this lean oasis at the moor's rim,
The marginal land where flesh meets spirit
Only on Sundays and the days between
Are mortgaged, mortgaged, mortgaged,
But we can see the faces of the men
Grouped together under the one lamp,
Waiting for the name to be born to them
Out of time's heaving thighs.

Did you dream, wanderer in the night,
Of the ruined house with the one light
Shining; and that you were the moth
Drawn relentlessly out of the dark?
The room was empty, but not for long.
You thought you knew them, but they always changed
To something stranger, if you looked closely
Into their faces. And you wished you hadn't come.
You wished you were back in the wide night
Under the stars. But when you got up to go
There was a hand preventing you.
And when you tried to cry out, the cry got stuck
In your dry throat, and you lay there in travail,
Big with your cry, until the dawn delivered you
And your cry was still-born and you arose and buried it,
Laying on it wreaths of the birds' songs.

But for some there is no dawn, only the light
Of the Cross burning up the long aisle
Of night; and for some there is not even that.

The cow goes round and round the field,
Bored with its grass world, and in its eyes
The mute animal hunger, which you pity,
You the confirmed sentimentalist,
Playing the old anthropomorphic game.
But for the cow, it is the same world over the hedge.
No one ever teased her with pictures of flyless meadows,
Where the grass is eternally green
No matter how often the tongue bruises it,
Or the dung soils it.

But with man it is otherwise.
His slow wound deepens with the years,
And knows no healing only the sharp
Distemper of remembered youth.

THE MINISTER

The Reverend Elias Morgan, B.A.:
I am the name on whom the choice fell.
I came in April, I came young
To the hill chapel, where long hymns were sung
Three times on a Sunday, but rarely between
By a lean-faced people in black clothes,
That smelled of camphor and dried sweat.

It was the time when curlews return
To lay their eggs in the brown heather.
Their piping was the spring's cadenza
After winter's unchanging tune.
But no one heard it, they were too busy
Turning the soil and turning the minister
Over and under with the tongue's blade.

My cheeks were pale and my shoulders bowed
With years of study, but my eyes glowed
With a deep, inner phthisic zeal,
For I was the lamp which the elders chose
To thaw the darkness that had congealed
About the hearts of the hill folk.

I wore a black coat, being fresh from college,
With striped trousers, and, indeed, my knowledge
Would have been complete, had it included
The bare moor, where nature brooded
Over her old, inscrutable secret.
But I didn't even know the names
Of the birds and the flowers by which one gets
A little closer to nature's heart.

Unlike the others my house had a gate
And railings enclosing a tall bush
Of stiff cypress, which the loud thrush
Took as its pulpit early and late.
Its singing troubled my young mind
With strange theories, pagan but sweet,
That made the Book's black letters dance
To a tune John Calvin never heard.
The evening sunlight on the wall
Of my room was a new temptation.
Luther would have thrown his Bible at it.
I closed my eyes, and went on with my sermon.

NARRATOR

A few flowers bloomed beneath the window,
Set there once by a kind hand
In the old days, a woman's gesture
Of love against the childless years.
Morgan pulled them up; they were untidy.
He sprinkled cinders there instead.

Who is this opening and closing the Book
With a bang, and pointing a finger
Before him in accusation?
Who is this leaning from the wide pulpit
In judgment, and filling the chapel
With sound as God fills the sky?
Is that his shadow on the wall behind?
Shout on, Morgan. You'll be nothing tomorrow.

The people were pleased with their new pastor;
Their noses dripped and the blood ran faster
Along their veins, as the hot sparks
Fell from his lips on their dry thoughts:
The whole chapel was soon ablaze.
Except for the elders, and even they were moved
By the holy tumult, but not extremely.
They knew better than that.

It was sex, sex, sex and money, money,
God's mistake and the devil's creation,
That took the mind of the congregation
On long journeys into the hills
Of a strange land, where sin was the honey
Bright as sunlight in death's hive.
They lost the parable and found the story,
And their glands told them they were still alive.
Job looked at Buddug, and she at him
Over the pews, and they knew they'd risk it
Some evening when the moon was low.

BUDDUG

I know the place, under the hedge
In the top meadow; it was where my mam
Got into trouble, and only the stars
Were witness of the secret act.
They say her mother was the same.
Well, why not? It's hard on a girl
In these old hills, where youth is short
And boys are scarce; and the ones we'd marry
Are poor or shy. But Job's got money,
And his wife is old. Don't look at me
Like that, Job; I'm trying to listen
To what the minister says. Your eyes
Scare me, yet my bowels ache
With a strange frenzy. This is what
My mother and her mother felt
For the men who took them under the hedge.

NARRATOR

The moor pressed its face to the window.
The clock ticked on, the sermon continued.
Out in the fir-tree an owl cried
Derision on a God of love.
But no one noticed, and the voice burned on,
Consuming the preacher to a charred wick.

THE MINISTER

I was good that night, I had the *hwyl*.
We sang the verses of the last hymn
Twice. We might have had a revival
If only the organ had kept in time.
But that was the organist's fault.
I went to my house with the light heart
Of one who had made a neat job
Of pruning the branches on the tree
Of good and evil. Llywarch came with me
As far as the gate. Who was the girl
Who smiled at me as she slipped by?

NARRATOR

There was cheese for supper and cold bacon,
Or an egg if he liked; all of them given
By Job Davies as part of his pay.
Morgan sat down in his white shirt-sleeves
And cut the bacon in slices the way
His mother used to. He sauced each mouthful
With tasty memories of the day.
Supper over, can you picture him there
Slumped in his chair by the red fire
Listening to the clock's sound, shy as a mouse,
Pattering to and fro in the still house?
The fire voice jars; there is no tune to the song
Of the thin wind at the door, and his nearest neighbour
Being three fields' breadth away, it more often seems
That bed is the shortest path to the friendlier morrow.

But he was not unhappy; there were souls to save;
Souls to be rescued from the encroaching wave
Of sin and evil. Morgan stirred the fire
And drove the shadows back into their corners.

THE MINISTER

I held a *seiat*, but no one came.
It was the wrong time, they said, there were the lambs,
And hay to be cut and peat to carry.
Winter was the time for that.
Winter is the time for easing the heart,
For swapping sins and recalling the days
Of summer when the blood was hot.
Ah, the blurred eye and the cold vein
Of age! 'Come home, come home. All is forgiven.'

I began a Bible class;
But no one came,
Only Mali, who was not right in the head.
She had a passion for me, and dreamed of the day . . .
I opened the Bible and expounded the Word
To the flies and spiders, as Francis preached to the birds.

NARRATOR

Over the moor the round sky
Was ripening, and the sun had spread
Its wings and now was heading south
Over the sea, where Morgan followed.
It was August, the holiday month
For ministers; they walked the smooth
Pavements of Aber and compared their lot
To the white accompaniment of the sea's laughter.

THE MINISTER

When I returned, strengthened, to the bare manse
That smelled of mould, someone had broken a window
During my absence and let a bird in.
I found it dead, starved, on the warm sill.
There is always the thin pane of glass set up between us
And our desires.
We stare and stare and stare, until the night comes
And the glass is superfluous.
I went to my cold bed saddened, but the wind in the tree
Outside soothed me with echoes of the sea.

Harvest, harvest! The oats that were too weak
To hold their heads up had been cut down
And placed in stooks. There was no nonsense
Plaiting the last sheaf and wasting time
Throwing sickles. That was fad of Prytherch
Of Nant Carfan; but the bugger was dead.
The men took the corn, the beautiful goddess,
By the long hair and threw her on the ground.

Below in the valleys they were thinking of Christmas;
The fields were all ploughed and the wheat in.
But Davies still hadn't made up his mind
Whom they should ask to the Thanksgiving.

The sea's tan had folded; the old pallor
Was back in Morgan's cheeks. In his long fight
With the bare moor, it was the moor that was winning.
The children came into Sunday School
Before he did, and put muck on his stool.
He stood for the whole lesson, pretending not to notice
The sounds in his desk: a mouse probably
Put there to frighten him. They loved their joke.
Say nothing, say nothing. Morgan was learning
To hold his tongue, the wisdom of the moor.
The pulpit is a kind of block-house
From which to fire the random shot
Of innuendo; but woe betide the man
Who leaves the pulpit for the individual
Assault. He spoke to Davies one day:

DAVIES

Adultery's a big word, Morgans: where's your proof?
You who never venture from under your roof
Once the night's come; the blinds all down
For fear of the moon's bum rubbing the window.
Take a word from me and keep your nose
In the Black Book, so it won't be tempted
To go sniffing where it's not wanted.
And leave us farmers to look to our own
Business, in case the milk goes sour
From your sharp talk before it's churned
To good butter, if you see what I mean.

NARRATOR

Did you say something?
Don't be too hard on them, there were people here
Before these and they were no better.
And there'll be people after may be, and they'll be
No better; it is the old earth's way
Of dealing with time's attrition.

Snow on the fields, snow on the heather;
The fox was abroad in the new moon
Barking. And if the snow thawed
And the roads cleared there was an election
Meeting in the vestry next the chapel.
Men came and spoke to them about Wales,
The land they lived in without knowing it,
The land that is reborn at such times.
They mentioned Henry Richard and S.R. – the great names;
And Keir Hardie; the names nobody knew.
It was quite exciting, but in the high marginal land
No names last longer than the wind
And the rain let them on the cold tombstone.
They stood outside afterwards and watched the cars
Of the speakers departing down the long road
To civilization, and walked home
Arguing confusedly under the stars.

THE MINISTER

Winter was like that; a meeting, a foxhunt,
And the weekly journey to market to unlearn
The lesson of Sunday. The rain never kept them
From the packed town, though it kept them from chapel.

Drive on, farmer, to market
With your pigs and your lean cows
To the town, where the dealers are waiting
And the girl in the green blouse,
Fresh as a celandine from the spring meadows,
Builds like a fabulous tale
Tower upon tower on the counter
The brown and the golden ale.

NARRATOR

A year passed, once more Orion
Unsheathed his sword from its dark scabbard;
And Sirius followed, loud as a bird
Whistling to eastward his bright notes.
The stars are fixed, but the earth journeys
By strange migrations towards the cold
Frosts of autumn from the spring meadows.
And we who see them, where have we been
Since last their splendour inflamed our mind
With huge questions not to be borne?

Morgan was part of the place now; he was beginning
To look back as well as forwards:
Back to the green valleys, forward along the track
That dwindled to nothing in the vast moor.
But life still had its surprises. There was the day
They found old Llywarch dead under the wall
Of the grey sheep-fold, and the sheep all in a ring
Staring, staring at the stiff frame
And the pursed lips from which no whistle came.

THE MINISTER

It was my biggest funeral of all; the hills crawled
With black figures, drawn from remote farms
By death's magnet. 'So sudden. It might have been me.'
And there in the cheap coffin Llywarch was lying,
Taller than you thought, and women were trying
To read through their tears the brass plate.

It might have been Davies! Quickly I brushed
The black thought away; but it came back.
My voice deepened; the people were impressed.
Out in the cold graveyard we sang a hymn,
O fryniau Caersalem; and the Welsh hills looked on
Implacably. It was the old human cry.
But let me be fair, let me be fair.
It was not all like this, even the moor
Has moods of softness when the white hair
Of the bog cotton is a silk bed
For dreams to lie on. There was a day

When young Enid of Gors Fach
Pressed an egg into my hand
Smiling, and her father said:
'Take it, Morgans, to please the child.'
I never heard what they said after,
But went to my bed that night happy for once.
I looked from my top window and saw the moon,
Mellow with age, rising over the moor;
There was something in its bland expression
That softened the moor's harshness, stifled the questions
Struggling to my lips; I made a vow,
As other men in other years have done,
Tomorrow would be different. I lay down
And slept quietly. But the morrow woke me
To the ancestral fury of the rain
Spitting and clawing at the pane.
I looked out on a grey world, grey with despair.

NARRATOR

The rhythm of the seasons: wind and rain,
Dryness and heat, and then the wind again,
Always the wind, and rain that is the sadness
We ascribe to nature, who can feel nothing.
The redwings leave, making way for the swallows;
The swallows depart, the redwings are back once more.
But man remains summer and winter through,
Rooting in vain within his dwindling acre.

THE MINISTER

I was the chapel pastor, the abrupt shadow
Staining the neutral fields, troubling the men
Who grew there with my glib, dutiful praise
Of a fool's world; a man ordained for ever
To pick his way along the grass-strewn wall
Dividing tact from truth.
                              I knew it all,
Although I never pried, I knew it all.
I knew why Buddug was away from chapel.

I knew that Pritchard, the *Fron*, watered his milk.
I knew who put the ferret with the fowls
In Pugh's hen-house. I knew and pretended I didn't.
And they knew that I knew and pretended I didn't.
They listened to me preaching the unique gospel
Of love; but our eyes never met. And outside
The blood of God darkened the evening sky.

NARRATOR

Is there no passion in Wales? There is none
Except in the racked hearts of men like Morgan,
Condemned to wither and starve in the cramped cell
Of thought their fathers made them.
Protestantism – the adroit castrator
Of art; the bitter negation
Of song and dance and the heart's innocent joy –
You have botched our flesh and left us only the soul's
Terrible impotence in a warm world.

Need we go on? In spite of all
His courage Morgan could not avert
His failure, for he chose to fight
With that which yields to nothing human.
He never listened to the hills'
Music calling to the hushed
Music within; but let his mind
Fester with brooding on the sly
Infirmities of the hill people.
The pus conspired with the old
Infection lurking in his breast.

In the chapel acre there is a grave,
And grass contending with the stone
For mastery of the near horizon,
And on the stone words; but never mind them:
Their formal praise is a vain gesture
Against the moor's encroaching tide.
We will listen instead to the wind's text
Blown through the roof, or the thrush's song
In the thick bush that proved him wrong,
Wrong from the start, for nature's truth
Is primary and her changing seasons
Correct out of a vaster reason
The vague errors of the flesh.

B

Children's Song

We live in our own world,
A world that is too small
For you to stoop and enter
Even on hands and knees,
The adult subterfuge.
And though you probe and pry
With analytic eye,
And eavesdrop all our talk
With an amused look,
You cannot find the centre
Where we dance, where we play,
Where life is still asleep
Under the closed flower,
Under the smooth shell
Of eggs in the cupped nest
That mock the faded blue
Of your remoter heaven.

The Village

Scarcely a street, too few houses
To merit the title; just a way between
The one tavern and the one shop
That leads nowhere and fails at the top
Of the short hill, eaten away
By long erosion of the green tide
Of grass creeping perpetually nearer
This last outpost of time past.

So little happens; the black dog
Cracking his fleas in the hot sun
Is history. Yet the girl who crosses
From door to door moves to a scale
Beyond the bland day's two dimensions.

Stay, then, village, for round you spins
On slow axis a world as vast
And meaningful as any posed
By great Plato's solitary mind.

Song at the Year's Turning

Shelley dreamed it. Now the dream decays.
The props crumble. The familiar ways
Are stale with tears trodden underfoot.
The heart's flower withers at the root.
Bury it, then, in history's sterile dust.
The slow years shall tame your tawny lust.

Love deceived him; what is there to say
The mind brought you by a better way
To this despair? Lost in the world's wood
You cannot stanch the bright menstrual blood.
The earth sickens; under naked boughs
The frost comes to barb your broken vows.

Is there blessing? Light's peculiar grace
In cold splendour robes this tortured place
For strange marriage. Voices in the wind
Weave a garland where a mortal sinned.
Winter rots you; who is there to blame?
The new grass shall purge you in its flame.

Invasion on the Farm

I am Prytherch. Forgive me. I don't know
What you are talking about; your thoughts flow
Too swiftly for me; I cannot dawdle
Along their banks and fish in their quick stream
With crude fingers. I am alone, exposed
In my own fields with no place to run
From your sharp eyes. I, who a moment back
Paddled in the bright grass, the old farm
Warm as a sack about me, feel the cold
Winds of the world blowing. The patched gate
You left open will never be shut again.

Taliesin 1952

I have been all men known to history,
Wondering at the world and at time passing;
I have seen evil, and the light blessing
Innocent love under a spring sky.

I have been Merlin wandering in the woods
Of a far country, where the winds waken
Unnatural voices, my mind broken
By sudden acquaintance with man's rage.

I have been Glyn Dŵr set in the vast night,
Scanning the stars for the propitious omen,
A leader of men, yet cursed by the crazed women
Mourning their dead under the same stars.

I have been Goronwy, forced from my own land
To taste the bitterness of the salt ocean;
I have known exile and a wild passion
Of longing changing to a cold ache.

King, beggar and fool, I have been all by turns,
Knowing the body's sweetness, the mind's treason;
Taliesin still, I show you a new world, risen,
Stubborn with beauty, out of the heart's need.

January

The fox drags its wounded belly
Over the snow, the crimson seeds
Of blood burst with a mild explosion,
Soft as excrement, bold as roses.

Over the snow that feels no pity,
Whose white hands can give no healing,
The fox drags its wounded belly.

Pisces

Who said to the trout,
You shall die on Good Friday
To be food for a man
And his pretty lady?

It was I, said God,
Who formed the roses
In the delicate flesh
And the tooth that bruises.

The Return

Coming home was to that:
The white house in the cool grass
Membraned with shadow, the bright stretch
Of stream that was its looking-glass;

And smoke growing above the roof
To a tall tree among whose boughs
The first stars renewed their theme
Of time and death and a man's vows.

A Welshman to Any Tourist

We've nothing vast to offer you, no deserts
Except the waste of thought
Forming from mind erosion;
No canyons where the pterodactyl's wing
Casts a cold shadow.
The hills are fine, of course,
Bearded with water to suggest age
And pocked with caverns,
One being Arthur's dormitory;
He and his knights are the bright ore
That seams our history,
But shame has kept them late in bed.

In a Country Church

To one kneeling down no word came,
Only the wind's song, saddening the lips
Of the grave saints, rigid in glass;
Or the dry whisper of unseeen wings,
Bats not angels, in the high roof.

Was he balked by silence? He kneeled long,
And saw love in a dark crown
Of thorns blazing, and a winter tree
Golden with fruit of a man's body.

No Through Road

All in vain. I will cease now
My long absorption with the plough,
With the tame and the wild creatures
And the man united with the earth.
I have failed after many seasons
To bring truth to birth,
And nature's simple equations
In the mind's precincts do not apply.

But where to turn? Earth endures
After the passing, necessary shame
Of winter, and the old lie
Of green places beckons me still
From the new world, ugly and evil,
That men pry for in truth's name.

POETRY FOR SUPPER
(1958)

Evans

Evans? Yes, many a time
I came down his bare flight
Of stairs into the gaunt kitchen
With its wood fire, where crickets sang
Accompaniment to the black kettle's
Whine, and so into the cold
Dark to smother in the thick tide
Of night that drifted about the walls
Of his stark farm on the hill ridge.

It was not the dark filling my eyes
And mouth appalled me; not even the drip
Of rain like blood from the one tree
Weather-tortured. It was the dark
Silting the veins of that sick man
I left stranded upon the vast
And lonely shore of his bleak bed.

Sailor Poet

His first ship; his last poem;
And between them what turbulent acres
Of sea or land with always the flesh ebbing
In slow waves over the salt bones.

But don't be too hard; so to have written
Even in smoke on such fierce skies,
Or to have brought one poem safely to harbour
From such horizons is not now to be scorned.

The Cat and the Sea

It is a matter of a black cat
On a bare cliff top in March
Whose eyes anticipate
The gorse petals;

The formal equation of
A domestic purr
With the cold interiors
Of the sea's mirror.

The Letter

And to be able to put at the end
Of the letter Athens, Florence – some name
That the spirit recalls from earlier journeys
Through the dark wood, seeking the path
To the bright mansions; cities and towns
Where the soul added depth to its stature.

And not to worry about the date,
The words being timeless, concerned with truth,
Beauty, love, misery even,
Which has its seasons in the long growth
From seed to flesh, flesh to spirit.

And laying aside the pen, dipped.
Not in tears' volatile liquid
But in black ink of the heart's well,
To read again what the hand has written
To the many voices' quiet dictation.

The View from the Window

Like a painting it is set before one,
But less brittle, ageless; these colours
Are renewed daily with variations
Of light and distance that no painter
Achieves or suggests. Then there is movement,
Change, as slowly the cloud bruises
Are healed by sunlight, or snow caps
A black mood; but gold at evening
To cheer the heart. All through history
The great brush has not rested,
Nor the paint dried; yet what eye,
Looking coolly, or, as we now,
Through the tears' lenses, ever saw
This work and it was not finished?

Ap Huw's Testament

There are four verses to put down
For the four people in my life,
Father, mother, wife

And the one child. Let me begin
With her of the immaculate brow
My wife; she loves me. I know how.

My mother gave me the breast's milk
Generously, but grew mean after,
Envying me my detached laughter.

My father was a passionate man,
Wrecked after leaving the sea
In her love's shallows. He grieves in me.

What shall I say of my boy,
Tall, fair? He is young yet;
Keep his feet free of the world's net.

The Journey

And if you go up that way, you will meet with a man,
Leading a horse, whose eyes declare:
There is no God. Take no notice.
There will be other roads and other men
With the same creed, whose lips yet utter
Friendlier greeting, men who have learned
To pack a little of the sun's light
In their cold eyes, whose hands are waiting
For your hand. But do not linger.
A smile is payment; the road runs on
With many turnings towards the tall
Tree to which the believer is nailed.

Poetry for Supper

'Listen, now, verse should be as natural
As the small tuber that feeds on muck
And grows slowly from obtuse soil
To the white flower of immortal beauty.'

'Natural, hell! What was it Chaucer
Said once about the long toil
That goes like blood to the poem's making?
Leave it to nature and the verse sprawls,
Limp as bindweed, if it break at all
Life's iron crust. Man, you must sweat
And rhyme your guts taut, if you'd build
Your verse a ladder.'
                              'You speak as though
No sunlight ever surprised the mind
Groping on its cloudy path.'

'Sunlight's a thing that needs a window
Before it enter a dark room.
Windows don't happen.'
                              So two old poets,
Hunched at their beer in the low haze
Of an inn parlour, while the talk ran
Noisily by them, glib with prose.

Meet the Family

John One takes his place at the table,
He is the first part of the fable;
His eyes are dry as a dead leaf.
Look at him and learn grief.

John Two stands in the door
Dumb; you have seen that face before
Leaning out of the dark past,
Tortured in thought's bitter blast.

John Three is still outside
Drooling where the daylight died
On the wet stones; his hands are crossed
In mourning for a playmate lost.

John All and his lean wife,
Whose forced complicity gave life
To each loathed foetus, stare from the wall,
Dead not absent. The night falls.

The Cure

But what to do? Doctors in verse
Being scarce now, most poets
Are their own patients, compelled to treat
Themselves first, their complaint being
Peculiar always. Consider, you,
Whose rough hands manipulate
The fine bones of a sick culture,
What areas of that infirm body
Depend solely on a poet's cure.

The Cry

Don't think it was all hate
That grew there; love grew there, too,
Climbing by small tendrils where
The warmth fell from the eyes' blue

Flame. Don't think even the dirt
And the brute ugliness reigned
Unchallenged. Among the fields
Sometimes the spirit, enchained

So long by the gross flesh, raised
Suddenly there its wild note of praise.

Bread

Hunger was loneliness, betrayed
By the pitiless candour of the stars'
Talk, in an old byre he prayed

Not for food; to pray was to know
Waking from a dark dream to find
The white loaf on the white snow;

Not for warmth, warmth brought the rain's
Blurring of the essential point
Of ice probing his raw pain.

He prayed for love, love that would share
His rags' secret; rising he broke
Like sun crumbling the gold air

The live bread for the starved folk.

Farm Wife

Hers is the clean apron, good for fire
Or lamp to embroider, as we talk slowly
In the long kitchen, while the white dough
Turns to pastry in the great oven,
Sweetly and surely as hay making
In a June meadow; hers are the hands,
Humble with milking, but still now
In her wide lap as though they heard
A quiet music, hers being the voice
That coaxes time back to the shadows
In the room's corners. O, hers is all
This strong body, the safe island
Where men may come, sons and lovers,
Daring the cold seas of her eyes.

TARES
(1961)

Walter Llywarch

I am, as you know, Walter Llywarch,
Born in Wales of approved parents,
Well goitred, round in the bum,
Sure prey of the slow virus
Bred in quarries of grey rain.

Born in autumn at the right time
For hearing stories from the cracked lips
Of old folk dreaming of summer,
I piled them on to the bare hearth
Of my own fancy to make a blaze
To warm myself, but achieved only
The smoke's acid that brings the smart
Of false tears into the eyes.

Months of fog, months of drizzle;
Thought wrapped in the grey cocoon
Of race, of place, awaiting the sun's
Coming, but when the sun came,
Touching the hills with a hot hand,
Wings were spread only to fly
Round and round in a cramped cage
Or beat in vain at the sky's window.

School in the week, on Sunday chapel:
Tales of a land fairer than this
Were not so tall, for others had proved it
Without the grave's passport, they sent
The fruit home for ourselves to taste.

Walter Llywarch – the words were a name
On a lost letter that never came
For one who waited in the long queue
Of life that wound through a Welsh valley.
I took instead, as others had done
Before, a wife from the back pews
In chapel, rather to share the rain
Of winter evenings, than to intrude
On her pale body; and yet we lay
For warmth together and laughed to hear
Each new child's cry of despair.

Genealogy

I was the dweller in the long cave
Of darkness, lining it with the forms
Of bulls. My hand matured early,

But turned to violence: I was the man
Watching later at the grim ford,
Armed with resentment; the quick stream

Remembers at sunset the raw crime.
The deed pursued me; I was the king
At the church keyhole, who saw death

Loping towards me. From that same hour
I fought for right, with the proud chiefs
Setting my name to the broad treaties.

I marched to Bosworth with the Welsh lords
To victory, but regretted after
The white house at the wood's heart.

I was the stranger in the new town,
Whose purse of tears was soon spent;
I filled it with a solider coin

At the dark sources. I stand now
In the hard light of the brief day
Without roots, but with many branches.

The Face

I see his face pressed to the wind's pane,
Staring with cold eyes: a country face
Without beauty, yet with the land's trace
Of sadness, badness, madness. I knew when
I first saw him that was the man
To turn the mind on, letting its beam
Discover rottenness at the seams
Of the light's garment I found him in.

Did I look long enough or too long?
On the weak brow nature's ruthless course
Was charted, but the lips' thin song
Never reached me; rain's decrepit hearse
Carried him off in the slow funeral
Of all his kind, leaving the heart full.

Anniversary

Nineteen years now
Under the same roof
Eating our bread,
Using the same air;
Sighing, if one sighs,
Meeting the other's
Words with a look
That thaws suspicion.

Nineteen years now
Sharing life's table,
And not to be first
To call the meal long
We balance it thoughtfully
On the tip of the tongue,
Careful to maintain
The strict palate.

Nineteen years now
Keeping simple house,
Opening the door
To friend and stranger;
Opening the womb
Softly to let enter
The one child
With his huge hunger.

Judgment Day

Yes, that's how I was,
I know that face,
That bony figure
Without grace
Of flesh or limb;
In health happy,
Careless of the claim
Of the world's sick
Or the world's poor;
In pain craven –
Lord, breathe once more
On that sad mirror,
Let me be lost
In mist for ever
Rather than own
Such bleak reflections.
Let me go back
On my two knees
Slowly to undo
The knot of life
That was tied there.

Hireling

Cars pass him by; he'll never own one.
Men won't believe in him for this.
Let them come into the hills
And meet him wandering a road,
Fenced with rain, as I have now;
The wind feathering his hair;
The sky's ruins, gutted with fire
Of the late sun, smouldering still.

Nothing is his, neither the land
Nor the land's flocks. Hired to live
On hills too lonely, sharing his hearth
With cats and hens, he has lost all
Property but the grey ice
Of a face splintered by life's stone.

C

Poet's Address to the Businessmen

Gentlemen all
At the last crumbfall,
The set of glasses,
The moist eye,
I rise to speak
Of things irrelevant:
The poem shut,
Uneasy fossil,
In the mind's rock;
The growth of winter
In the thick wood
Of history; music
We might have heard
In the heart's cloisters.
I speak of wounds
Not dealt us; blows
That left no bruises
On the white table
Cloth. Forgive me
The tongue's failure,
In all this leanness
Of time, to arrive
Nearer the bone.

Those Others

A gofid gwerin gyfan
Yn fy nghri fel taerni tân.
DEWI EMRYS

I have looked long at this land,
Trying to understand
My place in it – why,
With each fertile country
So free of its room,
This was the cramped womb
At last took me in
From the void of unbeing.

Hate takes a long time
To grow in, and mine
Has increased from birth;
Not for the brute earth
That is strong here and clean
And plain in its meaning
As none of the books are
That tell but of the war

Of heart with head, leaving
The wild birds to sing
The best songs; I find
This hate's for my own kind,
For men of the Welsh race
Who brood with dark face
Over their thin navel
To learn what to sell;

Yet not for them all either,
There are still those other
Castaways on a sea
Of grass, who call to me,
Clinging to their doomed farms;
Their hearts though rough are warm
And firm, and their slow wake
Through time bleeds for our sake.

Lore

Job Davies, eighty-five
Winters old, and still alive
After the slow poison
And treachery of the seasons.

Miserable? Kick my arse!
It needs more than the rain's hearse,
Wind-drawn, to pull me off
The great perch of my laugh.

What's living but courage?
Paunch full of hot porridge,
Nerves strengthened with tea,
Peat-black, dawn found me

Mowing where the grass grew,
Bearded with golden dew.
Rhythm of the long scythe
Kept this tall frame lithe.

What to do? Stay green.
Never mind the machine,
Whose fuel is human souls.
Live large, man, and dream small.

Mother and Son

At nine o'clock in the morning
My son said to me:
Mother, he said, from the wet streets
The clouds are removed and the sun walks
Without shoes on the warm pavements.
There are girls biddable at the corners
With teeth cleaner than your white plates
The sharp clatter of your dishes
Is less pleasant to me than their laughter.
The day is building; before its bright walls
Fall in dust, let me go
Beyond the front garden without you
To find glasses unstained by tears,
To find mirrors that do not reproach
My smooth face; to hear above the town's
Din life roaring in the veins.

A Welsh Testament

All right, I was Welsh. Does it matter
I spoke the tongue that was passed on
To me in the place I happened to be,
A place huddled between grey walls
Of cloud for at least half the year.
My word for heaven was not yours.
The word for hell had a sharp edge
Put on it by the hand of the wind
Honing, honing with a shrill sound
Day and night. Nothing that Glyn Dŵr
Knew was armour against the rain's
Missiles. What was descent from him?

Even God had a Welsh name:
We spoke to him in the old language;
He was to have a peculiar care
For the Welsh people. History showed us
He was too big to be nailed to the wall
Of a stone chapel, yet still we crammed him
Between the boards of a black book.

Yet men sought us despite this.
My high cheek-bones, my length of skull
Drew them as to a rare portrait
By a dead master. I saw them stare
From their long cars, as I passed knee-deep
In ewes and wethers. I saw them stand
By the thorn hedges, watching me string
The far flocks on a shrill whistle.

And always there was their eyes' strong
Pressure on me: You are Welsh, they said;
Speak to us so; keep your fields free
Of the smell of petrol, the loud roar
Of hot tractors; we must have peace
And quietness.

           Is a museum
Peace? I asked. Am I the keeper
Of the heart's relics, blowing the dust
In my own eyes? I am a man;
I never wanted the drab rôle
Life assigned me, an actor playing
To the past's audience upon a stage
Of earth and stone; the absurd label
Of birth, of race hanging askew
About my shoulders. I was in prison
Until you came; your voice was a key
Turning in the enormous lock
Of hopelessness. Did the door open
To let me out or yourselves in?

Here

I am a man now.
Pass your hand over my brow,
You can feel the place where the brains grow.

I am like a tree,
From my top boughs I can see
The footprints that led up to me.

There is blood in my veins
That has run clear of the stain
Contracted in so many loins.

Why, then, are my hands red
With the blood of so many dead?
Is this where I was misled?

Why are my hands this way
That they will not do as I say?
Does no God hear when I pray?

I have nowhere to go.
The swift satellites show
The clock of my whole being is slow.

It is too late to start
For destinations not of the heart.
I must stay here with my hurt.

The Maker

So he said then: I will make the poem,
I will make it now. He took pencil,
The mind's cartridge, and blank paper,
And drilled his thoughts to the slow beat

Of the blood's drum; and there it formed
On the white surface and went marching
Onward through time, while the spent cities
And dry hearts smoked in its wake.

The Survivor

Yesterday I found one left:
Eighty-five, too old for mischief.
What strange grace lends him a brief
Time for repenting of his theft
Of health and comeliness from her
Who lay caught in his strong arms
Night by night and heard the farm's
Noises, the beasts' moan and stir?

The land's thug: seventeen stone,
Settling down in a warm corner
By a wood fire's lazy purr;
A slumped bundle of fat and bone,
Bragging endlessly of his feats
Of strength and skill with the long scythe,
Of gallantry among the blithe
Serving women, all on heat

For him, of course. My mind went back
Sombrely to that rough parish,
Lovely as the eye could wish
In its green clothes, but beaten black
And blue by the deeds of dour men
Too like him, warped inside
And given to watching, sullen-eyed,
Love still-born, as it was then.

Wake him up. It is too late
Now for the blood's foolish dreaming.
The veins clog and the body's spring
Is long past; pride and hate
Are the strong's fodder and the young.
Old and weak, he must chew now
The cud of prayer and be taught how
From hard hearts huge tears are wrung.

THE BREAD OF TRUTH
(1963)

Funeral

They stand about conversing
In dark clumps, less beautiful than trees.
What have they come here to mourn?
There was a death, yes; but death's brother,
Sin, is of more importance.
Shabbily the teeth gleam,
Sharpening themselves on reputations
That were firm once. On the cheap coffin
The earth falls more cleanly than tears.
What are these red faces for?
This incidence of pious catarrh
At the grave's edge? He has returned
Where he belongs; this is acknowledged
By all but the lonely few
Making amends for the heart's coldness
He had from them, grudging a little
The simple splendour of the wreath
Of words the church lays on him.

Sorry

Dear parents,
I forgive you my life,
Begotten in a drab town,
The intention was good;
Passing the street now,
I see still the remains of sunlight.

It was not the bone buckled;
You gave me enough food
To renew myself.
It was the mind's weight
Kept me bent, as I grew tall.

It was not your fault.
What should have gone on,
Arrow aimed from a tried bow
At a tried target, has turned back,
Wounding itself
With questions you had not asked.

The Garden

It is a gesture against the wild,
The ungovernable sea of grass;
A place to remember love in,
To be lonely for a while;
To forget the voices of children
Calling from a locked room;
To substitute for the care
Of one querulous human
Hundreds of dumb needs.

It is the old kingdom of man.
Answering to their names,
Out of the soil the buds come,
The silent detonations
Of power wielded without sin.

The Untamed

My garden is the wild
   Sea of the grass. Her garden
Shelters between walls.
    The tide could break in;
    I should be sorry for this.

There is peace there of a kind,
   Though not the deep peace
Of wild places. Her care
    For green life has enabled
    The weak things to grow.

Despite my first love,
   I take sometimes her hand,
Following strait paths
    Between flowers, the nostril
    Clogged with their thick scent.

The old softness of lawns
   Persuading the slow foot
Leads to defection; the silence
    Holds with its gloved hand
    The wild hawk of the mind.

But not for long, windows,
   Opening in the trees
Call the mind back
    To its true eyrie; I stoop
    Here only in play.

The Boy's Tale

Skipper wouldn't pay him off,
Never married her;
Came home by Port Said
To a Welsh valley;
Took a girl from the tip,
Sheer coal dust
The blue in her veins.
Every time I go now
Through black sunlight,
I see her scratch his name
On the pane of her breath.
Caught him in her thin hair,
Couldn't hold him –
Voices from the ports
Of the stars, pavilions
Of unstable water.
She went fishing in him;
I was the bait
That became cargo,
Shortening his trips,
Waiting on the bone's wharf.
Her tongue ruled the tides.

Souillac: Le Sacrifice d'Abraham

And he grasps him by the hair
With innocent savagery.
And the son's face is calm;
There is trust there.

And the beast looks on.

This is what art could do,
Interpreting faith
With serene chisel.
The resistant stone
Is quiet as our breath,
And is accepted.

On the Farm

There was Dai Puw. He was no good.
They put him in the fields to dock swedes,
And took the knife from him, when he came home
At late evening with a grin
Like the slash of a knife on his face.

There was Llew Puw, and he was no good.
Every evening after the ploughing
With the big tractor he would sit in his chair,
And stare into the tangled fire garden,
Opening his slow lips like a snail.

There was Huw Puw, too. What shall I say?
I have heard him whistling in the hedges
On and on, as though winter
Would never again leave those fields,
And all the trees were deformed.

And lastly there was the girl:
Beauty under some spell of the beast.
Her pale face was the lantern
By which they read in life's dark book
The shrill sentence: God is love.

PIETÀ
(1966)

Pietà

Always the same hills
Crowd the horizon,
Remote witnesses
Of the still scene.

And in the foreground
The tall Cross,
Sombre, untenanted,
Aches for the Body
That is back in the cradle
Of a maid's arms.

Kierkegaard

And beyond the window Denmark
Waited, but refused to adopt
This family that wore itself out
On its conscience, up and down
In the one room.
                Meanwhile the acres
Of the imagination grew
Unhindered, though always they paused
At that labourer, the indictment
Of whose gesture was a warped
Crucifix upon a hill
In Jutland. The stern father
Looked at it and a hard tear
Formed, that the child's frightened
Sympathy could not convert
To a plaything.
                He lived on,
Søren, with the deed's terrible lightning
About him, as though a bone
Had broken in the adored body
Of his God. The streets emptied
Of their people but for a girl
Already beginning to feel
The iron in her answering his magnet's
Pull. Her hair was to be
The moonlight towards which he leaned
From darkness. The husband stared
Through life's bars, venturing a hand
To pluck her from the shrill fire
Of his genius. The press sharpened
Its rapier; wounded, he crawled
To the monastery of his chaste thought
To offer up his crumpled amen.

Ravens

It was the time of the election.
The ravens loitered above the hill
In slow circles; they had all air
To themselves. No eyes were lifted
From the streets, no ears heard
Them exulting, recalling their long
History, presidents of the battles
Of flesh, the sly connoisseurs
Of carrion; desultory flags
Of darkness, saddening the sky
At Catraeth and further back,
When two, who should have been friends,
Contended in the innocent light
For the woman in her downpour of hair.

The Moor

It was like a church to me.
I entered it on soft foot,
Breath held like a cap in the hand.
It was quiet.
What God was there made himself felt,
Not listened to, in clean colours
That brought a moistening of the eye,
In movement of the wind over grass.

There were no prayers said. But stillness
Of the heart's passions – that was praise
Enough; and the mind's cession
Of its kingdom. I walked on,
Simple and poor, while the air crumbled
And broke on me generously as bread.

There

They are those that life happens to.
They didn't ask to be born
In those bleak farmsteads, but neither
Did they ask not. Life took the seed
And broadcast it upon the poor,
Rush-stricken soil, an experiment
In patience.
                    What is a man's
Price? For promises of a break
In the clouds; for harvests that are not all
Wasted; for one animal born
Healthy, where seven have died,
He will kneel down and give thanks
In a chapel whose stones are wrenched
From the moorland.
                              I have watched them bent
For hours over their trade,
Speechless, and have held my tongue
From its question. It was not my part
To show them, like a meddler from the town,
Their picture, nor the audiences
That look at them in pity or pride.

The Belfry

I have seen it standing up grey,
Gaunt, as though no sunlight
Could ever thaw out the music
Of its great bell; terrible
In its own way, for religion
Is like that. There are times
When a black frost is upon
One's whole being, and the heart
In its bone belfry hangs and is dumb.

But who is to know? Always,
Even in winter in the cold
Of a stone church, on his knees
Someone is praying, whose prayers fall
Steadily through the hard spell
Of weather that is between God
And himself. Perhaps they are warm rain
That brings the sun and afterwards flowers
On the raw graves and throbbing of bells.

Aside

Take heart, Prytherch.
Over you the planets stand,
And have seen more ills than yours.
This canker was in the bone
Before man bent to his image
In the pool's glass. Violence has been
And will be again. Between better
And worse is no bad place

For a labourer, whose lot is to seem
Stationary in traffic so fast.
Turn aside, I said; do not turn back.
There is no forward and no back
In the fields, only the year's two
Solstices, and patience between.

The Visit

She was small;
Composed in her way
Like music. She sat
In the chair I had not
Offered, smiling at my left
Shoulder. I waited on
For the sentences her smile
Sugared.
        That the tongue
Is a whip needed no
Proving. And yet her eye
Fondled me. It was clear
What anger brought her
To my door would not unleash
The coils. Instead she began
Rehearsing for her
Departure. As though ashamed
Of a long stay, she rose,
Touched the tips of my cold
Hand with hers and turned
To the closed door. I remember
Not opening it.

The Face

When I close my eyes, I can see it,
That bare hill with the man ploughing,
Corrugating that brown roof
Under a hard sky. Under him is the farm,
Anchored in its grass harbour;
And below that the valley
Sheltering its few folk,
With the school and the inn and the church,
The beginning, middle and end
Of their slow journey above ground.

He is never absent, but like a slave
Answers to the mind's bidding,
Endlessly ploughing, as though autumn
Were the one season he knew.
Sometimes he pauses to look down
To the grey farmhouse, but no signals
Cheer him; there is no applause
For his long wrestling with the angel
Of no name. I can see his eye
That expects nothing, that has the rain's
Colourlessness. His hands are broken
But not his spirit. He is like bark
Weathering on the tree of his kind.

He will go on; that much is certain.
Beneath him tenancies of the fields
Will change; machinery turn
All to noise. But on the walls
Of the mind's gallery that face
With the hills framing it will hang
Unglorified, but stern like the soil.

In Church

Often I try
To analyse the quality
Of its silences. Is this where God hides
From my searching? I have stopped to listen,
After the few people have gone,
To the air recomposing itself
For vigil. It has waited like this
Since the stones grouped themselves about it.
These are the hard ribs
Of a body that our prayers have failed
To animate. Shadows advance
From their corners to take possession
Of places the light held
For an hour. The bats resume
Their business. The uneasiness of the pews
Ceases. There is no other sound
In the darkness but the sound of a man
Breathing, testing his faith
On emptiness, nailing his questions
One by one to an untenanted cross.

NOT THAT HE BROUGHT FLOWERS
(1968)

Careers

Fifty-two years,
most of them taken in
growing or in the
illusion of it – what does the mem-
ory number as one's
property? The broken elbow?
the lost toy? The pain has
vanished, but the soft flesh
that suffered it is mine still.

There is a house with
a face mooning at the glass
of windows. Those eyes – I look
at not with them, but something of
their melancholy I
begin to lay claim to as my own.

A boy in school:
his lessons are
my lessons, his
punishments I learn to deserve.
I stand up in him,
tall as I am
now, but without per-
spective. Distant objects
are too distant, yet will arrive
soon. How his words
muddle me; how my deeds
betray him. That is not
our intention; but where I should
be one with him, I am one now
with another. Before I had time
to complete myself, I let her share
in the building. This that I am
now – too many
labourers. What is mine is

not mine only; her love, her
child wait for my slow
signature. Son, from the mirror
you hold to me I turn
to recriminate. That likeness
you are at work upon – it hurts.

No

And one said, This man can sing;
Let's listen to him. But the other,
Dirt on his mind, said, No, let's
Queer him. And the first, being weak,
Consented. So the Thing came
Nearer him, and its breath caused
Him to retch, and none knew why.
But he rested for one long month,
And after began to sing
For gladness, and the Thing stood,
Letting him, for a year, for two;
Then put out its raw hand
And touched him, and the wound took
Over, and the nurses wiped off
The poetry from his cracked lips.

St Julian and the Leper

Though all ran from him, he did not
Run, but awaited
Him with his arms
Out, his ears stopped
To his bell, his alarmed
Crying. He lay down
With him there, sharing his sores'
Stench, the quarantine
Of his soul; contaminating
Himself with a kiss,
With the love that
Our science has disinfected.

Concession

Not that he brought flowers
Except for the eyes' blue,
Perishable ones, or that his hands,
Famed for kindness were put then
To such usage; but rather that, going
Through flowers later, she yet could feel
These he spared perhaps for my sake.

Shrine at Cape Clear

She is more white than the sea's
Purest spray, and colder
To touch. She is nourished
By salt winds, and the prayers
Of the drowned break on her. She smiles
At the stone angels, who have turned
From the sea's truth to worship
The mystery of her dumb child.

The bay brings her the tribute
Of its silences. The ocean has left
An offering of the small flowers
Of its springs; but the men read,
Beyond the harbour on the horizon,
The fury of its obituaries.

The Fisherman

A simple man,
He liked the crease on the water
His cast made, but had no pity
For the broken backbone
Of water or fish.

One of his pleasures, thirsty,
Was to ask a drink
At the hot farms;
Leaving with a casual thank you,
As though they owed it him.

I could have told of the living water
That springs pure.
He would have smiled then,
Dancing his speckled fly in the shallows,
Not understanding.

After the Lecture

I am asking the difficult question. I need help.
I'm not asking from ill will.
I have no desire to see you coping
Or not coping with the unmanageable coils
Of a problem frivolously called up.
I've read your books, had glimpses of a climate
That is rigorous, though not too hard
For the spirit. I may have grown
Since reading them; there is no scale
To judge by, neither is the soul
Measurable. I know all the tropes
Of religion, how God is not there
To go to; how time is what we buy
With his absence, and how we look
Through the near end of the binocular at pain,
Evil, deformity, I have tried
Bandaging my sharp eyes
With humility, but still the hearing
Of the ear holds; from as far off as Tibet
The cries come.
                    From one not to be penned
In a concept, and differing in kind
From the human; whose attributes are the negations
Of thought; who holds us at bay with
His symbols, the opposed emblems
Of hawk and dove, what can my prayers win
For the kindred, souls brought to the bone
To be tortured, and burning, burning
Through history with their own strange light?

Sailor's Hospital

It was warm
Inside, but there was
Pain there. I came out
Into the cold wind
Of April. There were birds
In the brambles' old,
Jagged iron, with one striking
Its small song. To the west,
Rising from the grey
Water, leaning one
On another were the town's
Houses. Who first began
That refuse: time's waste
Growing at the edge
Of the clean sea? Some sailor,
Fetching up on the
Shingle before wind
Or current, made it his
Harbour, hung up his clothes
In the sunlight; found women
To breed from – those sick men
His descendants. Every day
Regularly the tide
Visits them with its salt
Comfort; their wounds are shrill
In the rigging of the
Tall ships.
        With clenched thoughts,
That not even the sky's
Daffodil could persuade
To open, I turned back
To the nurses in their tugging
At him, as he drifted
Away on the current
Of his breath, further and further,
Out of hail of our love.

Reservoirs

There are places in Wales I don't go:
Reservoirs that are the subconscious
Of a people, troubled far down
With gravestones, chapels, villages even;
The serenity of their expression
Revolts me, it is a pose
For strangers, a watercolour's appeal
To the mass, instead of the poem's
Harsher conditions. There are the hills,
Too; gardens gone under the scum
Of the forests; and the smashed faces
Of the farms with the stone trickle
Of their tears down the hills' side.

Where can I go, then, from the smell
Of decay, from the putrefying of a dead
Nation? I have walked the shore
For an hour and seen the English
Scavenging among the remains
Of our culture, covering the sand
Like the tide and, with the roughness
Of the tide, elbowing our language
Into the grave that we have dug for it.

The Priest

The priest picks his way
Through the parish. Eyes watch him
From windows, from the farms;
Hearts wanting him to come near.
The flesh rejects him.

Women, pouring from the black kettle,
Stir up the whirling tea-grounds
Of their thoughts; offer him a dark
Filling in their smiling sandwich.

Priests have a long way to go.
The people wait for them to come
To them over the broken glass
Of their vows, making them pay
With their sweat's coinage for their correction.

He goes up a green lane
Through growing birches; lambs cushion
His vision. He comes slowly down
In the dark, feeling the cross warp
In his hands; hanging on it his thought's icicles.

'Crippled soul', do you say? looking at him
From the mind's height; 'limping through life
On his prayers. There are other people
In the world, sitting at table
Contented, though the broken body
And the shed blood are not on the menu'.

'Let it be so', I say. 'Amen and amen'.

Kneeling

Moments of great calm,
Kneeling before an altar
Of wood in a stone church
In summer, waiting for the God
To speak; the air a staircase
For silence; the sun's light
Ringing me, as though I acted
A great rôle. And the audiences
Still; all that close throng
Of spirits waiting, as I,
For the message.
           Prompt me, God;
But not yet. When I speak,
Though it be you who speak
Through me, something is lost.
The meaning is in the waiting.

Tenancies

This is pain's landscape.
A savage agriculture is practised
Here; every farm has its
Grandfather or grandmother, gnarled hands
On the cheque-book, a long, slow
Pull on the placenta about the neck.
Old lips monopolise the talk
When a friend calls. The children listen
From the kitchen; the children march
With angry patience against the dawn.
They are waiting for someone to die
Whose name is as bitter as the soil
They handle. In clear pools
In the furrows they watch themselves grow old
To the terrible accompaniment of the song
Of the blackbird, that promises them love.

No, Señor

We were out in the hard country.
The railroads kept crossing our path,
Signed with important names,
Salamanca to Madrid,
Malaga to Barcelona.
Sometimes an express went by,
Tubular in the newest fashion;
The faces were a blurred frieze,
A hundred or so city people
Digesting their latest meal,
Over coffee, over a cigarette,
Discussing the news from Viet Nam,
Fondling imaginary wounds
Of the last war, honouring themselves
In the country to which they belonged
By proxy. Their landscape slipped by
On a spool. We saw the asses
Hobbling upon the road
To the village, no Don Quixote
Upon their backs, but all the burden
Of a poor land, the weeds and grasses
Of the mesa. The men walked
Beside them; there was no sound
But the hoarse music of the bells.

Coto Doñana

I don't know; ask the place.
It was there when we found it:
Sand mostly, and bushes, too;
Some of them with dry flowers.
The map indicates a lake;
We thought we saw it from the top
Of a sand-dune, but walking brought it
No nearer.
          There are great birds
There that stain the sand
With their shadows, and snakes coil
Their necklaces about the bones
Of the carrion. At night the wild
Boars plough by their tusks'
Moonlight, and fierce insects
Sing, drilling for the blood
Of the humans, whom time's sea
Has left there to ride and dream.

Look

Look, here are two cronies, let's
Listen to them as the wind
Creeps under their clothes and the rain
Mixes with the bright moisture
Of their noses. They are saying,
Each in his own way, 'I am dying
And want to live. I am alive
And wish to die'. And for the same
Reason, that they have no belief
In a God who made the world
For misery and for the streams of pain
To flow in. Mildew and pus and decay
They deal in, and feed on mucous
And wind, diet of a wet land. So
They fester and, met now by this tree,
Complain, voices of the earth, talking,
Not as we wanted it to talk,
Who have been reared on its reflections
In art or had its behaviour
Seen to. We must dip belief
Not in dew nor in the cool fountain
Of beech buds, but in seas
Of manure through which they squelch
To the bleakness of their assignations.

Art History

They made the grey stone
Blossom, setting it on a branch
Of the mind; airy cathedrals
Grew, trembling at the tip
Of their breathing; delicate palaces
Hung motionless in the gold,
Unbelievable sunrise. They praised
With rapt forms such as the blind hand
Dreamed, journeying to its sad
Nuptials. We come too late
On the scene, pelted with the stone
Flowers' bitter confetti.

The Small Window

In Wales there are jewels
To gather, but with the eye
Only. A hill lights up
Suddenly; a field trembles
With colour and goes out
In its turn; in one day
You can witness the extent
Of the spectrum and grow rich

With looking. Have a care;
This wealth is for the few
And chosen. Those who crowd
A small window dirty it
With their breathing, though sublime
And inexhaustible the view.

Again

What to do? It's the old boredom
Come again: indolent grass,
Wind creasing the water
Hardly at all; a bird floating
Round and round. For one hour
I have known Eden, the still place
We hunger for. My hand lay
Innocent; the mind was idle.

Nothing has changed; the day goes on
With its business, watching itself
In a calm mirror. Yet I know now
I am ready for the sly tone
Of the serpent, ready to climb
My branches after the same fruit.

Burgos

Nightingales crackled in the frost
At Burgos. The day dawned fiercely
On the parched land, on the fields to the east
Of the city, bitter with sage
And thistle. Lonely bells called
From the villages; no one answered
Them but the sad priests, fingering
Their beads, praying for the lost people
Of the soil. Everywhere were the slow
Donkeys, carrying silent men
To the mesa to reap their bundles
Of dried grass. In the air an eagle
Circled, shadowless as the God
Who made that country and drinks its blood.

Study

The flies walk upon the roof top.
The student's eyes are too keen
To miss them. The young girls walk
In the roadway; the wind ruffles
Their skirts. The student does not look.
He sees only the flies spread their wings
And take off into the sunlight
Without sound. There is nothing to do
Now but read in his book
Of how young girls walked in the roadway
In Tyre, and how young men
Sailed off into the red west
For gold, writing dry words
To the music the girls sang.

That

It will always win.
Other men will come as I have
To stand here and beat upon it
As on a door, and ask for love,
For compassion, for hatred even; for anything
Rather than this blank indifference,
Than the neutrality of its answers, if they can be called, answers
These grey skies, these wet fields,
With the wind's winding-sheet upon them.

And endlessly the days go on
With their business. Lovers make their appearance
And vanish. The germ finds its way
From the grass to the snail to the liver to the grass.
The shadow of the tree falls
On our acres like a crucifixion,
With a bird singing in the branches
What its shrill species has always sung,
Hammering its notes home
One by one into our brief flesh.

The Place

Summer is here.
Once more the house has its
Spray of martins, Proust's fountain
Of small birds, whose light shadows
Come and go in the sunshine
Of the lawn as thoughts do
In the mind. Watching them fly
Is my business, not as a man vowed
To science, who counts their returns
To the rafters, or sifts their droppings
For facts, recording the wave-length
Of their screaming; my method is so
To have them about myself
Through the hours of this brief
Season and to fill with their
Movement, that it is I they build
In and bring up their young
To return to after the bitter
Migrations, knowing the site
Inviolate through its outward changes.

Index of Titles and First Lines

BLOODAXE BOOKS

POETRY WITH AN EDGE

HART CRANE
Complete Poems

One of America's most important poets. Lowell called Crane 'the Shelley of my age' and 'the great poet of that generation'. This new *Complete Poems*, based on Brom Weber's definitive 1966 edition, has 22 additional poems. *Sunday Times* Paperback of the Year.

JENI COUZYN (editor)
The Bloodaxe Book of Contemporary Women Poets*

Large selections – with essays on their work – by eleven leading British poets: Sylvia Plath, Stevie Smith, Kathleen Raine, Fleur Adcock, Anne Stevenson, Elaine Feinstein, Elizabeth Jennings, Jenny Joseph, Denise Levertov, Ruth Fainlight and Jeni Couzyn. Illustrated with photographs of the writers.

FRANCES HOROVITZ
Collected Poems*

'She has perfect rhythm, great delicacy and a rather Chinese yet very locally British sense of landscape . . . her poetry does seem to me to approach greatness' – PETER LEVI

MIROSLAV HOLUB
On the Contrary and Other Poems*
Translated by Ewald Osers

Miroslav Holub is Czechoslovakia's most important poet, and also one of her leading scientists. He was first introduced to English readers with a Penguin *Selected Poems* in 1967. This book presents a decade of new work. 'One of the half dozen most important poets writing anywhere' – TED HUGHES. 'One of the sanest voices of our time' – A. ALVAREZ

PETER DIDSBURY
The Butchers of Hull

'Peter Didsbury is a clever and original poet . . . He can be simultaneously knowing and naive, wittily deflationary yet alive to every leap of the post-Romantic eye . . . a soaring, playful imagination . . . I suspect that he is the best new poet that the excellent Bloodaxe Books have yet published' – William Scammell, TIMES LITERARY SUPPLEMENT

KEN SMITH
The Poet Reclining*

Ken Smith is a major British poet. *The Poet Reclining* was internationally acclaimed: 'A poet of formidable range and strength' (CHICAGO SUN-TIMES) . . . 'With Ken Smith we expect excellence . . . his achievement is remarkable' (SCOTSMAN) . . . 'Formidable, brilliant' (CITY LIMITS) . . . 'Compulsive, impressive' (LITERARY REVIEW) . . . 'Brilliant, impressive' (TLS).

SEAN O'BRIEN
The Indoor Park

Sean O'Brien won a Somerset Maugham Award and a Poetry Book Society Recommendation for *The Indoor Park*, his first collection of poems. 'I would back O'Brien as one of our brightest poetic hopes for the Eighties' – Peter Porter, OBSERVER

DAVID CONSTANTINE
Watching for Dolphins

Constantine's second book won him the Alice Hunt Bartlett Prize in 1984, and with it the judges' praise for 'a generous, self-aware sensuality which he can express in a dazzling variety of tones on a wide range of themes'. 'His imagination moves gracefully within the classical precincts of the pure lyric . . . There are some very beautiful poems in this collection' – George Szirtes, LITERARY REVIEW

PAUL HYLAND
The Stubborn Forest

'Paul Hyland has never written much like anyone else' (THE CUT). 'His is a rugged, hewn, earthbound poetry' (ENCOUNTER). 'Hyland's work has the character of primitive sculpture . . . an impressive, memorable and powerful talent' (NORTH). 'This is work of power and subtlety . . . *The Stubborn Forest* is a strikingly impressive achievement' (ANGLO-WELSH REVIEW). Winner of the 1985 Alice Hunt Bartlett Prize.

MARIN SORESCU
Selected Poems
Translated by Michael Hamburger

'Sorescu is already being tipped as a future Nobel prizewinner. His poems, however, have crowned him with the only distinction that matters. If you don't read any other new book of poetry this year, read this one' – William Scammell, SUNDAY TIMES

JOHN CASSIDY
Night Cries

'John Cassidy has produced a strong, delicate volume of nature poetry in *Night Cries*, sensitively alert to the mysterious unpredictability of natural things, lucid and tenaciously detailed . . . A kind of *Lyrical Ballads* of our time' – Terry Eagleton, STAND. Poetry Book Society Recommendation.

*Asterisked titles are available in hardback and paperback. Other books are in paperback only.

For a complete list of Bloodaxe publications, write to:
Bloodaxe Books Ltd, P.O. Box 1SN,
Newcastle upon Tyne NE99 1SN.